SoundByte Spirituality

SOUNDBYTE SPIRITUALITY:
sayings to awaken faith

by

Frank Sabatté
and Brett C. Hoover

Paulist Press
New York/Mahwah, N.J.

Copyright © 2002 by The Missionary Society of St. Paul the
Apostle in the State of New York

All rights reserved. No part of this book may be reproduced or transmitted in any form or by any means, electronic or mechanical, including photocopying, recording, or by any information storage and retrieval system without permission in writing from the Publisher.

Library of Congress Cataloging-in-Publication Data

Sabatté, Frank.
Soundbyte spirituality : sayings to awaken faith /
by Frank Sabatté and Brett C. Hoover.
p. cm.
ISBN 0-8091-4079-9
1. Spiritual life—Catholic Church. I. Hoover, Brett C. II. Title.
BX2350.3 .S23 2002
248.4'82—dc21
2002004485

Published by Paulist Press
997 Macarthur Boulevard
Mahwah, New Jersey 07430

www.paulistpress.com

Printed and bound in the
United States of America

cover by valerie petro
text by joseph e. petta

*For Ken McGuire
in friendship*

ON THE ART OF THE SOUNDBYTE...

At the very beginning of his work among the people of his country, Jesus of Nazareth appears to have given one of the shortest sermons on record. Most people are familiar with his longer sermons, such as the Sermon on the Mount or even the "Farewell Discourse" given on the night of the Last Supper as recorded in the Gospel of John. This shorter sermon is referred to in scholarly circles, interestingly enough, as Jesus' "inaugural address." In the original Greek of the New Testament, only nine words of it are recorded, usually nine words in the English translation as well. Here's how it happened:

> When [Jesus] came to Nazareth, where he had been brought up, he went to the synagogue on the sabbath day, as was his custom. He stood up to read, and the scroll of the prophet Isaiah was given to him. He unrolled the scroll and found the place where it was written:
>
> > "The Spirit of the Lord is upon me,
> > because he has anointed me
> > to bring good news to the poor.
> > He has sent me to proclaim release to the captives
> > and recovery of sight to the blind,
> > to let the oppressed go free,
> > to proclaim the year of the Lord's favor."

And he rolled up the scroll, gave it back to the attendant, and sat down. The eyes of all in the synagogue were fixed on him. Then he began to say to them, "Today this scripture has been fulfilled in your hearing."

Luke 4:16–21

In 1993 President Bill Clinton's inaugural address was over an hour in length, and his was by no means the longest on record. Here Jesus says nine words (he likely said a few more, but these were the key words remembered), and the following verse notes that "All spoke well of him and were amazed at the gracious words that came from his mouth" (Luke 4:22a). Later he said a few more words in response to their complimentary attitude, and in a few moments he was fleeing for his life!

The point is, more is not necessarily better. Sometimes just a few words, aptly said and well timed, can make an indelible impression. That's why there is a Bartlett's *Familiar Quotations* handbook. That's why we remember one-liners from movies, books, speeches, and friendly (and unfriendly) conversations. Many great heroes and heroines are remembered for their timely use of single, memorable phrases. Some stick in the memory as keys to visions and images. Martin Luther King says simply, "I have a dream," and everyone can tell you what that dream was about. Abe Lincoln says, "Whenever I hear anyone arguing for slavery, I feel a strong impulse to see it tried on him personally," and amidst laughter we know what he thought of slavery. In fact, humor is often precisely what catches us off guard and makes us think in these short statements. Incredibly, St. Lawrence quips as he is brutally roasted alive, "Turn me over; I think I'm done on this side." A harried Mother Teresa mutters, "I know God will not give me anything I can't handle—I just wish He didn't trust me so much."

Every now and then a single sentence, like a face, can launch a thousand ships. Newspapers crying out, "Remember the *Maine!*" struck such a chord in 1898 America that the country went to war with the battered and wounded Spain in the name of spurious and trumped-up charges of treachery in Havana harbor. The "soundbyte," as we now refer to such short, pithy locutions, has accomplished much evil in history, but it has also accomplished much good. Franklin Delano Roosevelt gives hope to a despairing nation suffering the Depression when he declares in his first inaugural address, "The only thing we have to fear is fear itself."

Overused and often disconnected from the substantive truths it once embodied, the soundbyte has fallen on hard times and deaf ears in our era. Madison Avenue and Hollywood search for the cleverest phrase of the moment without regard to what direction it might be pointing. Instead of being used to tweak the mind into examining a deep and complex truth, soundbytes are used to sell instant coffee and bad action movies. It's been cheapened, sold. It probably seems to many like it has no worth in the land of spirituality anymore.

But we have no such pessimism. Today perhaps like never before human minds are attuned to short, pithy phrases. In fact, they may have precious little patience and attention span for much more. If we can reattach soundbytes to spirituality in a way that sets us all thinking, then by God we have done something of value. Christian evangelicals have long been into this act, from the simplest of soundbytes, "Honk if you love Jesus," to the more sophisticated and contemporary, "In case of rapture, this car will be empty." It's past time for other Christian spiritualities to make their way into the soundbyte trade. We think soundbytes really can crack our minds open and make us think about things in a different way.

The sayings in this book (all of which are more or less original) are meant to jar your memory, jar it to the core, hopefully. In the old movies a running joke about the cure for amnesia was a second knock on the head, which, though not medically recommended, is along the lines of what we are trying to do here. Our suggestion: Keep this book nearby and read a line a day, or two or three as needed. Ponder the saying, flip it over in your mind a few times like a pancake; then apply it to your life, maybe even come up with one of your own. Add these sayings to your prayer, let them awaken your mind, bringing you back to Reality...you know, the One we know as the ever-present God who has never left us even on those occasions when we skipped town.

a collection of sayings

with commentary:

CHAPTER ONE

mystery

Spirituality:
> We walk
> > beyond the familiar
> > > into the chaos
> > > > of otherness where
> > > > > God dwells.

Human beings naturally want to move to their comfort zones. In the twentieth century in North America, there is more possibility for comfort than ever before in the history of human beings. Maybe too much. In the comfort zone, we are blissfully unaware and self-satisfied. We stop looking for God. We really can't see God at work in the world until something shakes us out of our counterproductive comfort.

**When I face myself
I face a Mystery
I cannot solve but one
I can embrace.**

At any given time in our lives we think we know who we are—but most of the time we come up short. At any given age in life much has been revealed—but not all of it. Can we embrace that and walk with the certain hope that more will be revealed, the wonder of which we can't even grasp?

**When God blesses us,
   it turns our world upside down—
which is good since we usually
   don't have it right side up.**

Only God's perspective is "right side up" always and everywhere. God gives us bits of this perspective from time to time, sometimes gently but often in ways that turn everything we know upside down. The starting of a relationship, the ending of one; finding a job, losing one; the birth of a baby, the death of a loved one: All are blessings for the person open to the new way of seeing what they offer.

Each life is a volume of sacred scriptures, unbound and unfinished but sacred, just like the version currently available at your bookstore.

Every life is a salvation history, a story of a journey with God and with humanity, which is why it is important to see all our experiences as religious experiences. Religious experiences are usually thought of as times of being lifted out of ordinary life, yet if that is true then few of us can claim such experiences. Religious experiences are when we see (suddenly or gradually) all our ordinary experiences but with a greater depth of field. Faith makes us do a double take, seeing more when we thought we had seen it all.

**The touch of another human being
is a taste of the Divine,
not the whole meal but a delicious taste.**

Human intimacy is as wonderful and delicious and life-changing as we experience it to be; it is that way because it reflects something greater: the Love of God. Relationships that last are those that have a transcendent reference, when you can embrace the Greater Love to which this great human love refers.

**Love desires to
   make us into Itself.
      All life is the attempt.**

God is Love, Love as verb, Love that is right now pulling at our humanity and making it stretch. All the events of our lives are God's way of making us more connected with all human beings at a soul level. If you let God form you through the events of your life, you find genuine kinship with more people, not less—a good test for spiritual practices.

**Spirituality is throwing darts at a dartboard—
and I always seem to hit just off the mark.**

God is always just a little beyond my imaginative and intellectual reach. So talking about faith, about our relationship with God, is an exercise in approximation. We coin metaphors. We make analogies. We draw pictures, ask questions, wonder aloud. And still we are off the mark. But that's good news. If we'd hit it exactly, we'd know for sure it wasn't God.

It's easy to try to do everything yourself, but only God can pull it off.

It is awfully hard for gifted, successful people to imagine just for a moment that they aren't God. When there's a tragedy and we get knocked off our feet, the door to our soul swings open and we pray, but as soon as the sadness fades we jump in our "God suit" and continue to be Masters of the Universe. The great spiritual traditions tell us that we are part of a greater Project, which Christianity calls the Kingdom. When we believe that, we find the joy of *being a part of* and lose the despair of *being apart from*.

**You can't
second-guess
another person because
you can't
second-guess
Mystery.**

Real relationships start when we see that this other person is Mystery unfolding. It might be that the best sign of the unfolding is the first fight, the first time you discover that the other person has warts. Even if you are with this person for fifty years, you will never understand him or her fully. Mystery is not meant to be understood but embraced in all its wonder.

**In trying to escape
    the awful awareness of being awake,
we miss the beauty
    of our vulnerable and blessed life.**

Being awake means facing the terror and joy of life as it is. At times I just don't feel like I have the faith to face up to the terror. But you can't have one without the other. I lose the sorrow and challenges—I also lose the joy and beauty. It's worth it to have both!

"Who is the woman clothed with the sun?" reads the inscription beside an image of Mary, the much-honored Mother of Jesus. The answer comes:
"I'm one of you. What exactly do you think *you're* wearing?"

It's natural to put our heroes and saints on pedestals. But we also have to recognize their *humanness* to learn for ourselves the qualities they represent. No one is more honored in many sectors of Christianity than Mary, the Mother of Jesus. Yet we honor her precisely because she is one of us. Her being chosen is our being chosen. Her destiny of glory is our destiny. Like that of Mary, our call is to uncover and allow God to complete what is divine in us.

**Nothing but God lasts forever—
 but we're all obsessed with the idea that there might be something else.**

No one has seen or touched God, though some have claimed to hear God's voice. The human heart reaches out instinctively, wants to be connected beyond itself. We reach out to other people, to material possessions, to projects and work and causes. None of this is bad, but all of it is transient, will pass away. Only God lasts forever. For the long haul the spiritual journey calls on us to see both the beauty in our awful limitations and the Source behind it all.

**What keeps me
   from knowing the intoxicating
       beauty of just being alive?**

Life is good. Or as the great teacher Rabbi Abraham Heschel used to say, "Just to be is blessing." As life's dark clouds appear over our heads, the temptation arrives to deny this, to close ourselves to the JOY of just being alive. Or even worse, in the pursuit of some ascetical religious nonsense, we begin to deny that creation is God's most glorious expression of love. We have to unlearn all this rejection of the glorious gift of life. God has loved us into being.

**To be
touched by
the Mystery of
another you must
let them go.**

The love we have for someone who has died does not diminish over time; it increases. Over time, a favorite picture or a letter brings us to ever deeper levels of awareness of the Mystery of this person, and, in fact, of their presence. The *communion of saints* in the Christian creed does not refer to a gathering far away; it points to a present reality, a *communion* that we have with those who have already been transformed, glorified. If Grandma loved us when she was alive, just imagine what she is doing now!

I will live with questions since God can be trusted.

As human beings, we want to make sense out of life. We want explanations and answers. We want to know what the "bottom line" is. What life hands us is questions: "Why am I here?" "What do I do with the rest of my life?" "Why did this accident have to happen?" The Bible even ends giving us many more questions than answers, contrary to popular fundamentalist stereotypes. Life is the process of great questions unfolding—answering themselves in our experience or becoming irrelevant as we grow. In other words, God lets us know at the proper time.

**After
everything
there
is
only
Silence.**

We are searching for the right words of comfort in this life, the highest number of *I love you*'s, the greatest amount of entertainment and liveliness. None of these things are wrong, but all of them are incomplete. What we must also develop a taste for is silence. There is a richness there that points the way to God.

CHAPTER TWO

love: god's obsession

Love is not about you.

This is hard to understand in our individualistic society. We are programmed to look first to our own care and comfort. But love calls us forth from ourselves, asks us to make decisions for another's good. The hardest times are the test of love—can we continue to give when a friend is sick, when a spouse is depressed, to children who are often unable to give back? God wants us to let go of our self-importance. Only by loving others do we learn how to love God.

The God of Love makes a mess of things in our lives— so we secretly wish that the atheists were right!

Sometimes we prefer "cozy religion"—religion that assures us that the world as we know it is just fine and will stay that way right up to "check-in" at the pearly gates. God loves us too much to let us settle for a tiny world (the world of our plans), so God steps in, shakes things up, rattles our cage. Somewhere deep inside we probably know this about God, which is why at times we might secretly wish that the atheists were right!

**Love
is like the
Hokey-Pokey—
sooner or later you
have to put your
whole self
in.**

One of the greatest fears most North Americans have today is of getting involved. Our model is business. We want to maximize our advantage while we minimize the risk of getting hurt. So our commitment proceeds to a level that is minimal for the task, safe. With relationships with people, as with God, this approach only brings us isolation and minimal human challenge. Love requires risk, challenge, even hurt. Without a more significant investment (there goes business again!), we will never experience the riches that love can bring.

The Kingdom can't depend on our mood swings.

Jesus did not command us to "like one another," he said: "Love one another." There is nothing wrong with liking someone, just don't confuse it with love. Liking someone focuses on what they do for you; loving someone is what you must do to honor who they are. When we are suffering we can lose our ability to like—the emotions become caught up in the pain—but we can still choose to do the loving thing. Liking does not require sacrifice, but loving always does.

**Blessings aren't the neat stuff we get;
blessings are what we get to figure out
what to do with all this neat stuff.**

People often point to what they have and call these things "blessings," but what about people who don't have a house or kids or spouse or a car or interest-bearing maximizer account—are they cursed? God throws good stuff all over the earth; some catch more of it than others, which means the challenge is what to do with it all. Blessings are all the skills, tools, creativity, and grace God gives to help us figure out what to do with all this good stuff so that everyone on the earth can feast. Blessings are what God gives us to help us get big hearts, not big houses.

**Daydreams and fantasies
are comfortable.
People are complex and scary.
But people make us grow.**

Daydreams and fantasies are tailor-made for our diversion and pleasure. That is why we love them! They give us the excitement and outcomes we crave, but in the comfort and protection of our own minds. As with everything, however, there is a danger. We can begin to prefer our imagined encounters with others over our actual encounters. After all, people are so unpredictable and unwilling to submit to our control. But it's only the topsy-turvy challenges of living in actual relationships with other human beings that causes us to grow!

Love does not calculate the chances of getting what I want.

People do a lot of calculating when they are in love: "Will she go out with me?" "What does he think about me?" Real love, love that reflects God's love, puts the focus on the other. Love is about seeing the other person's reality and honoring it. Not that you accept destructive behaviors, but intervening for the sake of another's life must start by accepting the other as a unique expression of the Eternal Mystery we call God.

**It is in God's own best interests
to look after us since
that means he's taking
good care of himself.**

Thomas Aquinas taught that each of us participates in the Being of God; it is who we are. When we hear, "God loves you," it can reinforce the notion of a nice but distant God who smiles down on us from time to time. God *is* Love and, as St. Augustine says, is "closer to us than we are to ourselves." The greatest proof of this are the ways God moves us to greater and greater solidarity with other human beings—with us kicking and screaming all the way!

**You can't touch God,
but you can let God teach
you how to touch.**

Jesus put love of God and love of neighbor together for a reason. God desires our good, and our good is shaped as a people. The Kingdom is humanity gathered around the table feasting with joy. For that you need to know how to touch people, and God is the only one who can teach you. In fact, God is probably teaching you right now.

Love is
holding someone's hand
even when you can't stand them.

If you don't think this is true, try being married, try having children, try just walking with your best friend through the moment when his or her worst qualities are brought out. No one is completely good. No one is completely nice. I wade through another's dark sides trusting that the good in them will win out and that he or she will be able to endure my particular brand of craziness.

**We wrestle with love
on our way to losing our terrible
self-importance.**

Relationships are a school of love. We find our way to truly valuing the good in others by struggling with the differences and conflicts, the joys and questions that relationships bring to us. Over time, we begin to lose our adolescent narcissism—life is not about me. We relativize our own concerns with the concerns of those we love and who depend on us. Sometimes we resent it for a while, but in the long run, we are better people.

**Being "pure"
doesn't mean avoiding life;
it means
having the courage to embrace it.**

For some people, being pure seems to mean a life of avoidance. There *are* dangers, toils, and snares out there, but the greatest danger is the danger of avoiding life instead of embracing it. "I have come that you may have life and have it abundantly," Jesus said (John 10:10). Purity of heart means having a heart that is free and capable of self-sacrificing love. A pure heart sees the goodness of life and trusts its Author and Sustainer, who made it very good indeed.

Premise 1: Everyone is the Beloved of God.

Premise 2: Not everyone is treated like the Beloved of God.

Therefore: Something has to give.

Jesus showed that all are the Beloved of God. He didn't say you will become the Beloved of God if you do x, y, and z or jump through approved religious hoops. Realizing that all human beings *are* the Beloved of God presents the challenge of having to inspect our whole society—all of its social, political, and religious structures—to make sure these structures reflect this truth, and for some of us that is a scary prospect.

You are God's obsession.

Spiritual writer Edward Farrell wrote years ago that a saint is someone who is convinced that God is in love with them. We hear in homily after homily that "God loves you," but only the saints and mystics know just how crazy in love God is. Maybe we avoid the realization because of our own human experience. When human beings fall in love, everything changes—so if we let God love us? Yikes!

CHAPTER THREE

pray or die

**In terms of getting
through the week,
here is the advice I give:
Pray or die.**

Prayer often seems like a boring extra duty—a repetitive task to be completed when work and family obligations allow me the time. But over time, a discipline of prayer reminds us simply that we can't do it on our own. Only God can get us out of our very human messes—addiction, anger, disappointments, fear, illness, anxiety, conflict. Ultimately, prayer is less a rote remembrance and more admitting to ourselves that we need God—that we won't be able to make it through the week without God.

**Prayer is
allowing yourself
to be directed by
a Power
greater than you.**

Far too often good people will take themselves to task for not praying enough or for not praying in the correct manner. There are many prayer *forms* but *prayer* is better understood as the ways we express what we believe in all aspects of our lives. Our relationship to God is expressed even more eloquently when we visit a sick neighbor or give the surly store clerk a kind word than when we talk to God alone in our room or in church.

We are comfortable *hearing*
   that each human being is made in the
   image and likeness of God,
   but treating him or her
       that way is another matter.

It's too easy to treat people as objects—the object of my business right now, the object of my message, sex object, and so on. It's hard to remember (sometimes especially with family members, ironically!) that each human being has his or her own thoughts, feelings, history, and dreams. Each one is beloved by God. Gracious God, let me love as you do!

If you are afraid of how God will answer your prayers, you are praying to something but it isn't the God of Jesus.

It may have been Jesus' biggest job to get people to reevaluate their concept of God and to act accordingly. How often do we pray to a benevolent dictator instead of the Abba who holds us in loving hands? But we might then jump to the conclusion that we need to get the "right" *concept* of God, which as St. Anselm taught us, we can never do. What we can do is trust the *Mystery* of God, a Mystery who has made his Presence known over and over in our lived experience.

**Hope is
that small tug
inside that gets you
out of bed.**

Never underestimate the grace involved in getting out of bed! Hope is a push from God, and its appearance does not rely on us except insofar as we are the only ones who can actually get ourselves out of bed—God can't do that for us! Awakening to the realization that we've been *pulled* out of despair (perhaps many times) is enough for us to do great things. That is hope.

Prayer is facing what is Real.

For some folks, prayer is escape—overcome with emotion I soar to 40,000 feet. In fact, we all have moments, safe in the privacy of our own minds, when we pray as if we had already reached the spiritual heights we hope for. Beware! God is what is most Real in the universe, and a part of inviting God in (i.e., prayer) is coming to terms with myself where I *really* am on the spiritual journey—stupidly scrambling to find my way like everybody else.

Having a vision
   means seeing something really neat
      once, maybe twice.
Having vision means seeing *everything*
   more clearly more of the time.

Who of us wouldn't want to have a vision? An apparition that would really get our attention. But the fact is that most of us don't have visions of the supernatural. We live and move and have our being in the world of *ordinary* people, places, and things. What faith does is enable us to see those ordinary people, places, and things differently. Each shock of grace that comes into our lives in both painful and joyful experiences can open our eyes such that we see everything and everyone in richer color and greater depth.

**Stop pretending
you've got it
together—God loves
the weak at least
as much as the
strong.**

I knew a man who couldn't pray until he cleaned his room. He wanted everything perfect for God. But God doesn't want our accomplishments—God wants us, as we are, warts and all. St. Paul said that "whenever I am weak, then I am strong" (2 Corinthians 12:10). When we recognize our weakness, we give up our pretensions to self-sufficiency and learn to lean on God.

Discipline is motor oil for the soul.

There is no accomplishment in any field without practice, and practice requires discipline. This is just as true with our faith and spirituality as it is with basketball or soccer. To really become whole (that is, holy) people, we need prayer, reflection on our lives, spiritual reading, ritual. Regularly.

**Prayer is
like looking at God
through a steamed window.**

God is Mystery. As soon as we start taking our images and thoughts of God to be unreservedly the real thing, we're in trouble. We do not yet see face to face with God. Better to recognize that we are following someone whose actions and presence can be detected but not understood or pinned down. We see the outlines without a clear look at God's face.

Pray from wherever you are standing.

In our secular times a lot of people don't know exactly where to begin when praying. Should I start with memorized prayers like the Lord's Prayer? Should I go for a half hour? An hour? Is it okay to use my own words? The best advice is not to worry too much about these things in the beginning. Instead, I start by reflecting on the circumstances of my life—Who am I most concerned about? What are my weaknesses? Strengths? What is happening in my heart on the deepest level? Start with these things, and God will take care of the rest.

**O Hidden One,
     can these nervous mumblings
          also be prayer?**

Okay, I don't have to be a perfect contemplative or an eloquent speaker to pray! God wants us to pray from the heart, letting out whatever it is that daunts us, whatever we face, whatever our hearts want to say. Many of us only like prayer if it is tidy and pleasant. God appreciates all prayers, more so when they are honest.

CHAPTER FOUR

god's will?!

Relying on your calculations to arrive in heaven may divert you to hell.

When we rely on our own calculations for a happy life, we are assuming that we have the scope to navigate the path to fulfillment all on our own. Then the plan hits a dead end—we despair, finding ourselves hiding in a dark place: hell....But there is a way out of hell: the way of surrender. Turning our lives over to God and allowing God to direct us out of that dark place will provide us with a new life on a new path—not of our design but one designed for us.

**Waiting for the expected miracle
 we often miss the ironic
  workings of the real God.**

Irony has to do with the reversal of expectations. It's pretty close to a definition of how God works. This is the God who calls old childless women (Sarah, Hannah, and Elizabeth) to be the mothers of patriarchs (Isaac) and prophets (Samuel and John the Baptist). This God makes the persecutor of Christians a great apostle (St. Paul), chooses a failed apostle as "rock" (St. Peter), and has a scrawny little shepherd boy anointed as king (King David). This God wants to shake things up, to upset our expectations so that we might let go of romanticized miracles and take hold of the real miracles of every day.

**God is building
the Kingdom;
what'll you do when
it's in your face?**

If you look around, it's pretty clear that a lot of people are doing a lot of good. God is doing God's work; the question is: When the invitation to be a part of this effort comes to us, what choice will we make? Will we get involved? When we are faced with the chance to forgive someone, what will we do? What opportunities are we being given not just to *help* the poor but to *get to know them?*

What you think God gives you depends on what you think of God.

If your image of God is of a monster, you will expect to get monstrous things. If, in the midst of a tragedy like the sudden death of a loved one, you think of God as a distant parent, unavailable, remote, then you will conclude that God is cruel and has given you suffering because you deserve it. If your God is Compassion, the God who is with you through thick and thin, that realization itself will be enough for you.

The truth will set you free, but only after upsetting you first.

"I am a lonely person," a man said aloud. It angered him that with all the many friends he had that this could still be true. He felt betrayed but also angry with himself for being satisfied with superficial relationships. He vowed to do differently after that, and he did. The truth set him free, unpleasant as it was.

Be careful about opening your heart. That's God's cue to rule it.

God's rule is not something "out there" imposed on people. God's rule isn't in competition with the deepest of our human desires, what we really want in our heart of hearts—the place from where God "rules" us. The problem is we are afraid to take the steps necessary to follow our heart of hearts. We close our hearts lest we hear the voice calling us to freedom and happiness, and we are faced with a decision of whether we really want to go there (meaning a whole new life).

**There are things
we want so much to be
real that we assume it so;
but that doesn't make them real.**

There is nearly always a difference between what we wish would be and what is. "I want peace in my family." "I wish that I could achieve my career dream now." Sometimes these desires can be so strong that we half-consciously block out the evidence to the contrary. We want peace in the family so much that we ignore all the signs that things are falling apart. But denial won't prevent the falling apart. And after all, spirituality means facing reality and letting it teach us. We suffer for it sometimes, but in the long run we become better people.

> Don't panic
> if you haven't changed
> the world yet—
> God is on the job.

Here in the United States we like to pride ourselves on what a little common sense and practicality can do. But changing the world is just a little beyond us. When we try to take on responsibility for *everything*, we often end up accomplishing little—setting ourselves up to fail. More than a few activists and idealists have lost their enthusiasm that way. Faith means we don't have to do it all ourselves. Ironically, by trusting God to direct the whole drama all the way to the end, we free ourselves to excel in the role each of us has been given.

**God is building the Kingdom—
have
your hard hat
ready
at all times.**

Be ready to respond to the invitation to build a better world. It might not be as big as a year with the poor in Calcutta (though it might); more likely it will be the opportunity to forgive someone who hurt you or to be an advocate for someone who is being unfairly treated at work. Whatever it is, it will come soon, because God never stops building.

CHAPTER FIVE

student of the master

A Christian is a lifelong student of Christ the Master; the trouble starts when we think we've graduated.

God will decide when we are done with our lessons, not us. Everything that happens to us in life is an opportunity to let the Master teach us something, open us up to new realizations, new awareness. But we have to want to learn, we have to remain teachable. That's why good friends don't help us by solving the lesson for us—good friends keep us from running away from school!

**Telling people you love Jesus
might
get you in trouble.
Living the message of Jesus
will
get you in trouble.**

Telling people you love Jesus might irritate them, but they probably won't kill you for saying it. If however you set out to bring justice to the poor and oppressed, if you love your enemies, if you question unjust structures (in other words, if you live the gospel of Jesus), you will, like Gandhi or Martin Luther King, Jr., or Archbishop Oscar Romero of El Salvador, get into trouble—guaranteed. No one likes his or her world rocked and no one will like *you* for rocking it.

Everybody is shouting out what they really believe—but only 2 percent of that is words.

Someone said: "You will defend to the death that which you most fully believe." Jesus knew that the heart has its ways of expressing its truth, which is why he insisted that genuine conversion had to go deep. If you are going to work for a better world, you better make sure it is coming from the *heart,* because regardless of your words, what is down there is what you will proclaim.

If you're not dressed for the journey, don't leave the house.

The spiritual life is just like the boy scouts. "Be prepared." Many times we say that we are interested in spirituality and are itching to embark on a journey toward greater faith and God-consciousness. But are we really ready to embark? The spiritual life requires discipline, a commitment to introspection, prayer, study, spiritual reading, contact with others on the journey. If we do not prepare ourselves for this journey of faith, we will soon find ourselves in over our heads!

**People
who love
Jesus
love people.
All people.**

You have to wonder if Christians who patronize or condemn people ever catch the contradiction. Anything we do that separates us from people, any resentments we hold, any prejudice, any fear, makes it impossible for us to understand Jesus. An accurate measure of an authentic spiritual life is the level of active compassion we have for others. If we are arrogant or hateful we can say we love Jesus, but whatever it is we love it sure isn't Jesus.

**Prophets don't depend
on fulfillment
in their jobs.
Pretenders insist on it.**

If a teacher makes his or her teaching pleasure more important than the students themselves, how can that teacher make a difference? How can he teach the hard lessons? How can she move the students from self-centeredness to other-centeredness? Prophets can speak the truth because they themselves have been freed by it and cannot bear the sight of any form of slavery. Great teachers are prophets, truth-tellers, and so are great parents and great friends.

Humility is a virtue that you cultivate over time. False modesty is a performance that you practice in front of the mirror.

The fundamental question here is: Who is life all about? If life is all about me (i.e., being the prince or princess), then it's perfectly reasonable to play the humble one for attention and advantage. But if life is about how we can all accomplish things together, then it is better for me to learn who I am and who I am not, to know what I have to offer to the community and what I need from others. That is humility, and it takes a lot of practice.

**Lots of
people want to
go to church; not a
lot of people want to
be a church.**

If you *are* a church, if you are the community of disciples that Jesus called together, you will have to get serious about the mission Jesus gave his followers: to go out and make the world a better place, a place of hearts open to being ruled by selfless Love. It is a hard mission, which is why a lot of people settle for church being the place you go to get spiritual comfort food.

The Lord is my shepherd:
'Cause *I* sure don't know where the pasture is.

Theologian Avery Dulles said, "A disciple by definition is someone who isn't finished yet." We forget that a disciple is a lifelong student of the Master. Jesus reminded Peter to "get back behind me" (Matt 16:23), when Peter insisted that his directions made more sense than the Lord's. Don't we Christians get into the most trouble when we claim we have arrived at clarity while the rest of humanity is to be pitied for their stupidity?

**A
real
prophet
has doubts
about her calling.**

All true prophets are called; they don't volunteer. And when they are called, they come up with all the reasons why they are inadequate to the task. But God calls them because they have a heart and a soul; they have what it takes to perceive what God is up to and point it out. False prophets are entertainers—they tell people what they want to hear. It is a very attractive job because you will always have an appreciative audience.

**Lesson of loaves and fishes:
As soon as we learn to be a *community*
instead of a crowd, we'll have all
the bread we'll ever need.**

There are several New Testament tales in which Jesus multiplies bread and fish so that deprivation becomes abundance. The lesson is about crowds and communities. A crowd is a group of individuals who happen to be interested in the same thing. A community is a people who are in communion with all humanity, who are joined to humanity in such a way that when one laughs all laugh, and when one cries all cry. In a crowd people worry about having enough to eat. In a community no one gives it a second thought.

**Christ is
one king you
have to ask
to rule
you.**

If you want Christ to rule your heart you have to ask; there is no way he will force his way in. If you want to become compassionate, forgiving, and merciful; if you want to be directed toward the Holy; you have to ask for it. Christ knocks on the door but never breaks it down—it's yours to open.

**Of all the gifts
    for a would-be grown-up,
Lord, give me humility.**

The beginning of wisdom is to admit our limitations—what we don't know, what we can't do, who we aren't. Humility has more to do with this and nothing at all to do with putting ourselves down. Putting ourselves down is as sinful as putting others down! Humility is simply recognizing who God is, who we are, and the difference between the two.

**We love saints
when they're smiling
on holy cards, but living
with them is another matter.**

There are living saints among us. You know you are close to saints when just being around them makes you see your own silly selfishness. Big hearts expose small hearts. God is trying to make all of us into saints, people with big hearts, transparent to the Love of God. If you want that to happen to you, then hang around the saints—otherwise run like hell!

**Advisory to those seeking heaven:
You will have to ask for directions.**

The mark of a Christian disciple is one who is eager to learn—not someone absolute in his or her convictions. To seek out the wise, put yourself at their feet, and listen—this is a good practice to learn at an early age. And it's the surest way to find heaven.

CHAPTER SIX

panic!

**We always fear
the wrong kind of disasters.**

Children believe in wish fulfillment—if what I wished for happens, I caused it. Adults believe in fear fulfillment—what I am afraid of will happen. And maybe it will, but it probably wasn't the real problem that needed my attention. There was a young couple who always feared their child would be kidnapped; in the meantime, their smothered child began to feel resentful. This was not what they feared, but sooner or later they would have to deal with it. The moral: Better to watch the signs around me and trust in God than build my life on fear!

**Panic
causes
spiritual amnesia.**

When we panic we forget everything. We forget every single time we have been saved from harm. We forget that the times when we were tempted to give in to despair, to believe our own worst fears and give up, God brought us through. In the old comedies the cure for amnesia was another knock on the head, which is what the Spirit sometimes has to do for us, too!

**Learning to read the
sacred scriptures
of your life
will save
your
life.**

Seeing the patterns of your life, having them sewn together and handed back to you as a marvelous quilt is the work of spiritual direction, which can be done formally or informally, individually or as a group. Seek out wise women and men of faith who can teach you how to read the Good Book of your life.

**Panic is
being caught in an endless
loop of
merely human solutions.**

When we panic, all we can see are dead ends, and our clever ideas fail us. Still we insist that we can solve this dilemma ourselves, and so we spin and spin and come up exhausted. Unchecked panic can lead to despair, but that won't happen unless we persist in repelling grace. God's grace reminds us that the dreadful conclusions we draw when we are panicked ought to be ignored.

**Hope is trusting
that when the credits roll,
life will have
turned out to be a good movie.**

It's tough to think long-term in life, but it helps a lot. In the long run what we want from our lives is not an easy life but a good life—one where we loved those who belonged to us, found a way to serve our communities, and left a positive imprint on the world we inhabited. Cynicism says it can't be done and recommends that we each just get as much personal pleasure and comfort out of life as we can. Hope says that we *can* do good—indeed, that it will also bring us contentment in the long run.

**It is
important
to remember
that we
forget.**

How many walks in cool of the Garden have we had with God (Genesis 3:8)? When did we have our breath taken away at the sight of a tiny baby? When did we experience intimate love? When did we feel we were with a Presence other than ourselves? Yet when we are hurt or fearful we forget those walks. The grace of community is that not everyone forgets at once! In our times of forgetfulness, if we place ourselves in the company of those who remember their walks with God, soon our memory will be restored. And we will be able to be a reminder for others.

Hope is the horizon of openness for all that will be.

Rather than face life with an impending sense of disaster, a Christian confronts life with a confidence that, come what may, God will bring good of it. This is not a naive acceptance of the status quo as God's will. It is an enduring trust that God can write straight with crooked lines, that the possibility of good lies at every next crossroad.

CHAPTER SEVEN

nonstop forgiveness

A summary of Jesus' entire teaching on forgiveness: Just do it!

Forgiveness isn't an emotion—it is a choice, a decision. When we have been hurt, a decision to forgive will be hard, but many serious decisions in life have to be made under intense and difficult circumstances. With God's help and the support of compassionate people, we can decide to forgive even while our wound is healing; in fact our decision will hasten the healing.

To forgive without whining: That is virtue!

The real task of a truly forgiving person is to forgive and forget—to let go of the resentments that accompany the hurt. We can't do this task alone, we have to ask God to take our resentments away so we can live in gratitude.

**Resentment gives you
    all the energy you need to keep your
world comfortable and familiar and
    very much like hell.**

Resentments can be exciting. It's negative excitement but excitement nevertheless—which may be why we don't like letting go of them. After we've had a resentment for a while, it becomes a familiar piece of furniture; we know our way around it. Losing our resentment means the end of the world, the world as we know it, but it also means getting out of our isolated hell and entering the Kingdom of God.

**To forgive is to "give before"—
    before worship can be real.**

Jesus told us to reconcile with our brother or sister before we go to worship. How much heartfelt praise can we give God if our heart is tied up with grudges? No sacrament can penetrate the hard shell of resentment. We can go to church every week but never really worship until we realize that real forgiveness *is* real worship.

If forgiving someone requires waiting until you feel good about it, have a seat, 'cause you're going to have a long wait.

You will hear people say that they aren't ready to forgive someone or that they need to be "in a good space" before they do so. Emotions take time to heal, and we need to take time for the spiritual and psychological work of healing. But some wounds take a lifetime to heal, which, for the sake of our own serenity, is too long to wait to forgive. Get with those who have a proven track record as good forgivers and follow their lead!

Salt of the earth:
   You are a flavoring for
      What Really Matters.

What really matters? Justice, peace, compassion, a world where people forgive seventy times seven times (Matthew 18:21–22), where no one starves to death and where all praise the Creator with every breath. Each of us is called to be the salt for that banquet; each lesson in mercy and forgiveness we practice brings zest to the meal.

You know you are becoming a Christian when the elapsed time between the perceived offense and heartfelt forgiveness becomes shorter and shorter.

People who are really good at forgiveness know how to let go of a hurt quickly. They have no place in their hearts for vengeance because they would rather use all available space for love. Getting good at forgiveness, then, takes a lifetime of practice, following the example of good teachers, starting with Jesus himself.

**Only a pure heart can see God.
Only when forgiveness
is as constant as your
breath will you gain a pure heart.**

Ever wonder how much of life we miss while we are holding on to resentments or when we are full of anger? A lot. Resentments can run deep and hide out in our souls, coloring all our perceptions; they can even appear justified. Forgiveness is a daily practice to improve our perception of reality, to see more of the sacred that surrounds us.

> There is always someone you don't need to forgive for a "good" reason, except that there aren't any good reasons not to forgive.

The argument that executing a criminal will deter crime sounds rational and has society's blessing, but it is really saying that there are limits to forgiveness. Jesus clearly put no limits on forgiveness (Matthew 18:22; Luke 23:34). God will give us what we need to do the work of forgiveness if we are only willing to ask.

**You
forgive to
save your own soul,
not to change
someone
else's.**

When we ask forgiveness of someone, our work is finished the moment we make our amends—not after the person accepts it, since it may not work out that way. If I expect asking for forgiveness will suddenly make someone a better friend to me or convince them to let go of the hurt, I could be disappointed. Learning how to forgive is my work. God will give the one I forgive the opportunity to learn how in God's own time.

As long as we consider anyone a stranger we have not understood the meaning of forgiveness.

When Jesus told the crowd about to stone the adulteress, "Let anyone among you who is without sin be the first to throw a stone at her" (John 8:7), he was giving the people there an opportunity to see their relatedness to the woman and to all humanity. We must live as a forgiving people to insure that we never become a mob with stones at the ready.

CHAPTER EIGHT

cashing in on suffering

One of the great
        and most
   important lessons of life
       is how to
             suffer well.

American society is obsessed with staying comfortable. From air conditioning to pizza delivery to videos, we seek convenience. Yet so much of life, as the Buddha taught, is suffering. Do we teach our children how to suffer well? Do we encourage them to share with others what ails them? Do we show them how to do that without gathering undue attention to themselves? Do we flat-out tell them that God will get them through? Aren't these some of the most important lessons to pass on?

**Another
of the great lessons of life
is how to hold
    suffering and gratitude
in the same heart.**

When you learn how to hold suffering and gratitude in your heart, your heart grows big, so big that other people start to notice it before you do. Of course, holding these two together in your heart requires learning from people who know how to do it. But they are easy to find…if you want to find them.

The Lord is my shepherd but still I whine!

The saints who have gone before us and the saints among us don't sit around and complain all the time, which is what whining is, which is why it is a good idea to spend some time among saints. You can find them without too much trouble. Look for older women and men who have suffered a lot and who seem to ooze love out of every pore. Their every other sentence contains "thanks be to God."

Pagan gods pass their time *watching* people live. The God of Jesus is busy *showing* people how.

God doesn't live on Mount Olympus; God doesn't gaze on us from afar. We live in God; we are God's heart. Pagan gods are aloof and arrogant; the God of Jesus is Compassion itself right in the thick of the action.

**We think God is
comfort or happiness,
but God is
whatever leads us to love.
Isn't that
often suffering?**

For decades now, we've heard the "positive thinking" gurus and preachers. Happiness is supposed to be our right, comfort our goal. But the God of Judaism, Christianity, and Islam has always been associated with justice, mercy, and love. Surely whatever builds up these qualities in our lives is of God. Very often it is the uncomfortable things of life—conflict, vulnerability, anger, hurt—that teach us to love better, to seek justice, to be merciful.

**Everything in life is gift.
It's not *ever* about deserving.**

Are you trying to earn your way to salvation? Take this simple test: (1) Do you think God will love you only if you work really hard? (2) Are you uncomfortable when someone loves you just for who you are? It's time to stop! Every moment that we have of life, every person that we call friend, everything that we have in our possession, every opportunity we are granted—all these are God's gift to us, and we can't possibly earn it. God's way is the way of grace, of no-strings-attached generosity.

**Give up the
   "if only"
fantasies and
   just hurt—
grief leads us to peace.**

Fantasies are not wrong. Who could live without them? But sometimes, pressed by grief or anger or anguish at the unjust way life has turned out, we resort to some fantasy to hide the pain. I pretend it's really okay. I imagine a different outcome where I don't get hurt. Yet eventually we all have to hurt, to grieve, to endure the awful weight of loss. And then time passes and we heal. And we learn we are stronger than we thought!

**Suffering
is the
classroom
of
compassion.**

Those still unharmed by life think they can be compassionate, but their compassion often fades before what is disturbing and hard to fathom. When we suffer, we begin to learn how to do it well and how to comfort others in the process of it. We hurt and we recover, over and over again. Through this process we learn how difficult life really can be—and we become less tempted to judge others and more tempted to empathize.

Give your suffering to God and be amazed what God does with it.

Suffering isn't an option—it is a fact of life. The question is: What are you going to do with it? Jesus taught us that what you give to God, God will make into something worthwhile that can benefit others. If you keep it to yourself, you become bitter. But in God's hands, wounds become more precious than gold.

World says:
>God allowed this bad thing
>to happen to you.

Faith says:
>God is getting you through this bad
>thing that's happening to you.

Believe what the world says and you will become bitter—there is no other way. Choose what faith says and you will become wise and joyful and free. You probably know people who hang on to the notion that God let this bad thing happen to them—they aren't fun to be around. You probably also know people who believe that God got them through what happened. And I bet you come alive around them.

**The truth will set you free,
free from illusion—
which will mean the end of the world
as you knew it—
but you could probably use a
new world anyway.**

The truth hurts, but only because it's sad to see our familiar ideas and beliefs go. They've become like old shoes, comfortable but useless for further walking. The new world that truth opens up to us is scary, but only because it is unknown. Yet if we recall, we've stepped into the unknown before. Haven't we learned by now that what we expect is seldom what we find?

**Sometimes our fear
of being abandoned is
exactly what makes us search for
God in silence.**

Many of us are afraid of being left alone in life, some because of difficult childhood experiences. But the truth is, another human being or even a community of others cannot possibly fill all our voids, heal all our wounds, satisfy all our needs. And the resulting restlessness is often what leads us straight to God. When there's nowhere to go, there's only one place left...God!

CHAPTER NINE

faith

Faith is taking a step forward even when you don't know what you're stepping in.

You never do know what you're stepping in. Life is uncertain. No one can predict what is around the corner. This truth often leads us to fearful anxiety or hiding where life is comfortable. But faith means trusting that God will take care of me in the midst of life's twists and turns and my own bad decisions. So go ahead, take that step. It leads to growth and more life!

World says:
>What you see is what you get.

Faith says:
>You don't see what you've got.

Faith does not make us see a different reality from everyone else; it helps us see the present reality with greater clarity. Faith improves our sight so that, over the course of a faithful life, we become more related to all human beings; we see the intensity of the beauty of creation and the hand of God in every moment of every life.

**We are monotheists
in training—
not quite ready to put our trust
in God alone.**

Forget pagan idols. Forget Ba'al. Forget mother goddesses. The real polytheism in our time involves the gods we actually bow to: drugs and alcohol, success in business, the person of our obsessions, comfort, sex, work, collecting toys, whatever. We all have conflicted loyalties, and yet each one of us is called to give our ultimate allegiance to the God who is beyond our imaginings. This is hard. It's much easier to put our trust in success. But success isn't forever, no matter how much the economy is expanding. Sex isn't forever, no matter how good it is. Work can't buy us meaning for all time. Everyone has to retire. As St. Teresa said, "Only God is enough."

In our grief we try to punish God by not believing in him.

When we lose someone or something that means a lot to us, we go into a time of grief (whether we admit it or not). Part of grief is anger, often directed at God. Some of us were taught that anger is wrong, especially directed at God. Yet the anger remains inside of us; maybe the only way to express it is to shut God out. "I refuse to believe in you because you let this happen." But it's a temporary solution. God is not so easy to get rid of!

Some people say it's
    too hard to trust through
        a time of doubt—but do you
give up at night thinking day
    will never come?

Time is the test of all things. Cycles come and go. People marry to pass through good times and bad times. Grief strikes for a period of months and then eases up. No time of doubt or darkness will last forever. We have to pray for patience and let go of our awful sense of tragedy. The universe is not arrayed against us. Life is merely difficult, meant for our learning as much as for our enjoyment.

**You start to see
when you
admit
you are
blind.**

The great spiritual traditions teach that if you want spiritual awareness you have to admit you know nothing and see nothing and have everything to learn, and that only God can teach you. You will only see something of the Reality that surrounds you when you can admit that your attempts to grasp it, define it, capture it, have failed, and you are open, finally open to a Reality and a Plan greater than yours.

**Going to church is about
     being reminded that we
          have work to do when we
  aren't going to church.**

Sometimes we don't like being reminded that the work begins when we head out the door of the church. Complaints rain in when the preacher raises issues of social justice or unpacks the meaning of "love your enemies." But the gospel is supposed to be a way of life, not empty words. A church of the comfortable won't be very interested in taking risks, which is what we have to do if we want to follow Jesus.

**If you
have to wait
until you feel better
before you care, you won't care.**

The amazing thing about service to others is not only are people served, but miraculous things happen to the souls of those who serve. Service opens us, moves us, expands us, which is why we can't wait until we feel better about ourselves before we serve. We may have too long a wait and our soul is just too important to leave at a pity party.

World says:
> Life should be easy or it's your fault.

Faith says:
> Life is God's work—and it's not done till you're done.

The notion that life should be easy is based on an inability to see life's struggles as having any value. The hard things of life can make us bitter, or they can make us wise. We become bitter when we allow the berating voices from the past to direct us to isolation. We become wise when we let the Spirit stirring deep in our heart direct us to others. They can help us and we can help them, gradually making us all into people who put compassion, forgiveness and love back into the world.

> We live, we love, we die.
> With faith in God
> maybe that is
> more than
> enough.

Part of the process of growing up is letting go of my delusions of grandeur. This is not to say I am no longer ambitious. Rather, I try not to let my self-esteem ride on the accomplishment of all my dreams. Life is in itself a precious, amazing gift. Sometimes, dreaming of great things, a person can forget to note its wonder and forget to give thanks. Beyond that, there is no greater human gift than the opportunity to love and be loved by others. Why would I want anything more than life and love?

The last good test for
    genuine faith is that in the end after
you've survived it all you give
    the credit to God.

All we have is pure gift. Our life, our faith, everything is gift, a truth we have the hardest time remembering. Like the Israelites newly freed from slavery in Egypt, we are much better at grumbling than praising, which is why we need saints and prophets around to remind us where credit is due.

SPECIAL ACKNOWLEDGMENTS:

For the "dartboard" soundbyte on page 15, the authors wish to thank Warren Holmes.

For the "truth" soundbyte on page 61, the authors thank Ken McGuire.